CELESTIAL ANGEL

HONEY

ANGEL, I'M SOMEBODY'S ANNIE?

3

BEGINNER ANGEL

Test
Pattern

5

Test Pattern

9

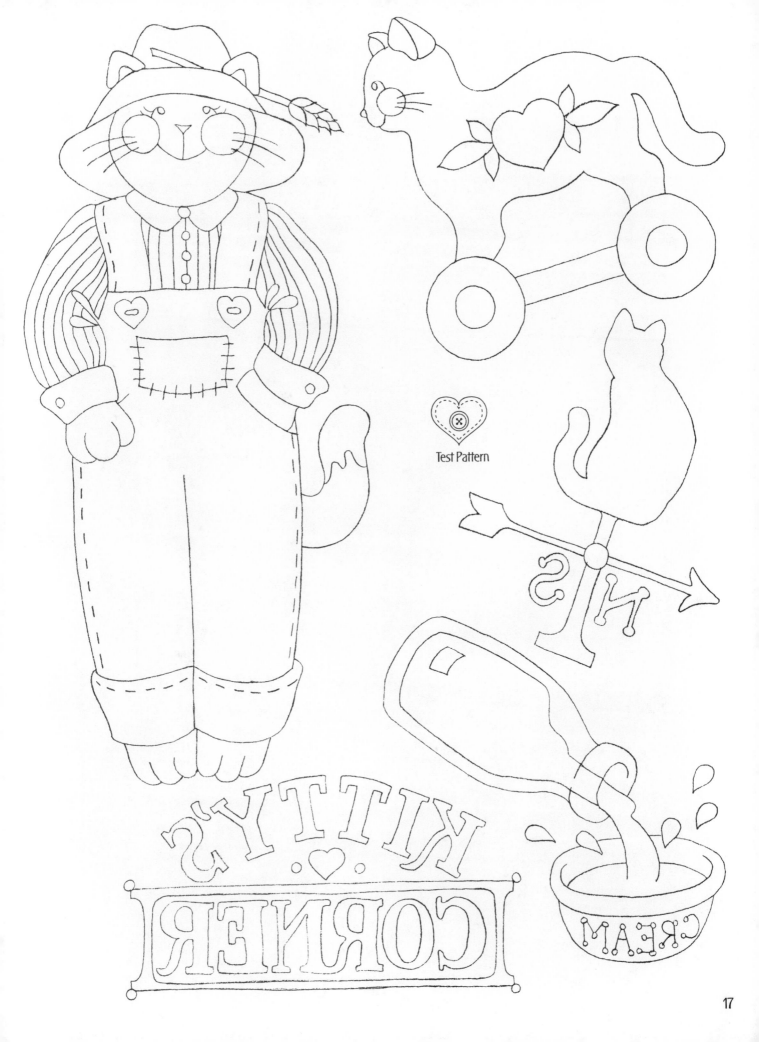

Test Pattern

KITTY'S CORNER

CREAM

17

Test
Pattern

21

Test Pattern

Test
Pattern

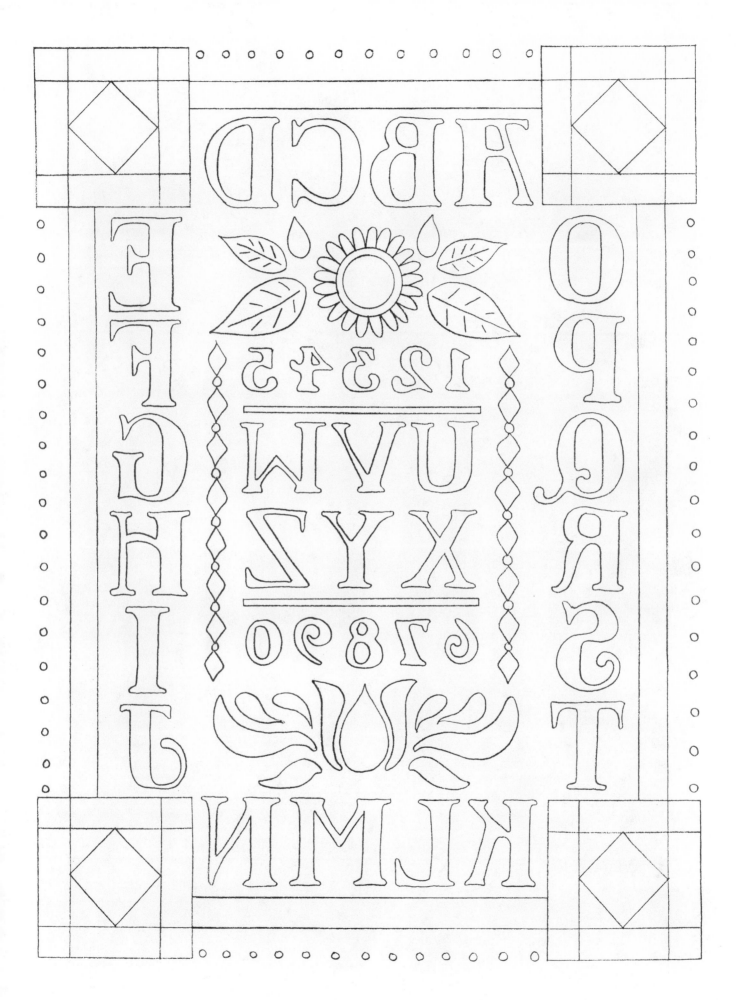

Test
Pattern

37

Test Pattern

EAT YOUR
CARROTS!

buttons

Test
Pattern

a stitch in
time saves
NiNE

Test Pattern

49

TRICK or TREAT

51

Test
Pattern

53

HAPPY EASTER

I ♥ EASTER

Test Pattern

COUNTRY HOME

I LOVE

MY

THE HERD IS WHERE MOM IS

59

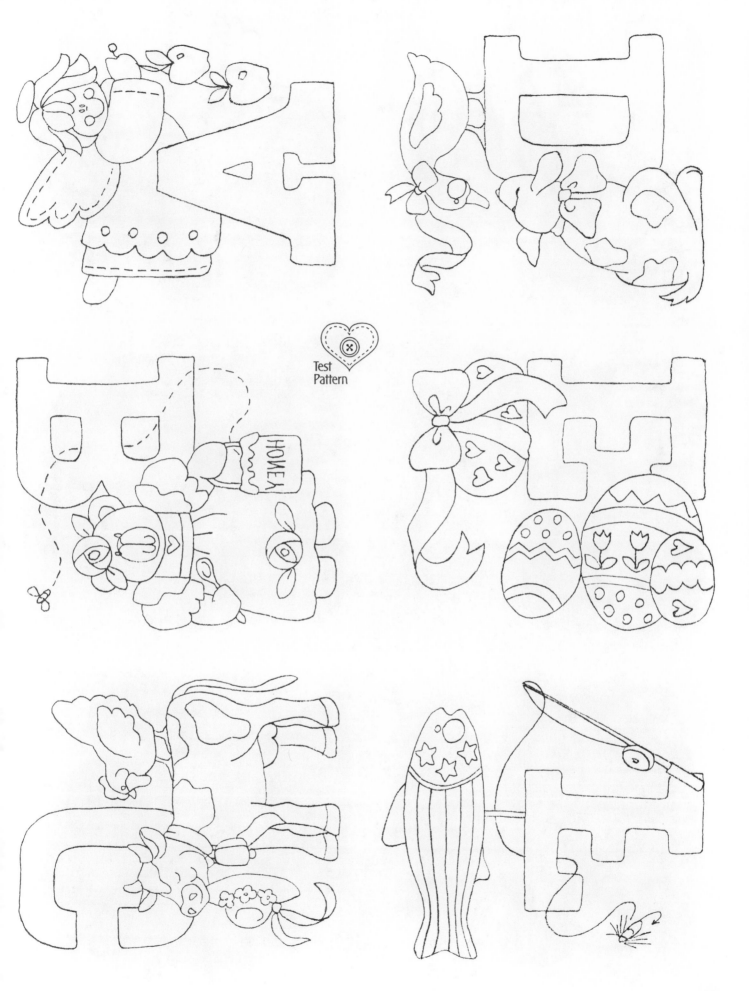

Test
Pattern

Test Pattern

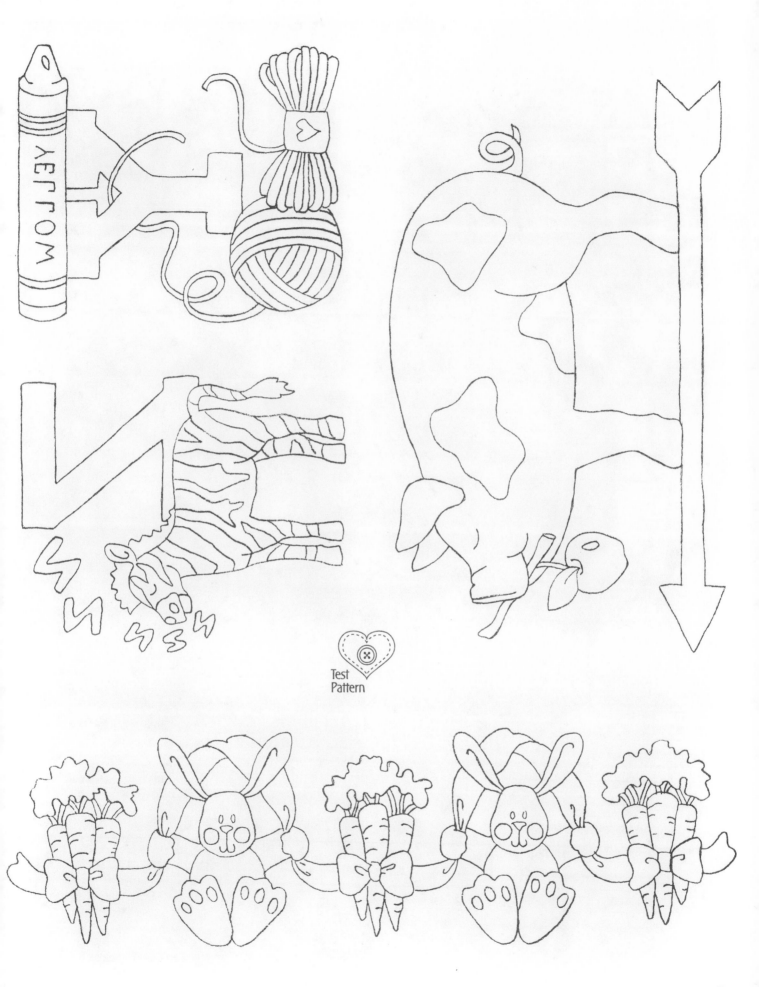

YELLOW

Test
Pattern

69

LOVE BLOOMS HERE

PLANT
SEEDS OF LOVE

LOVE SEEDS

Test Pattern

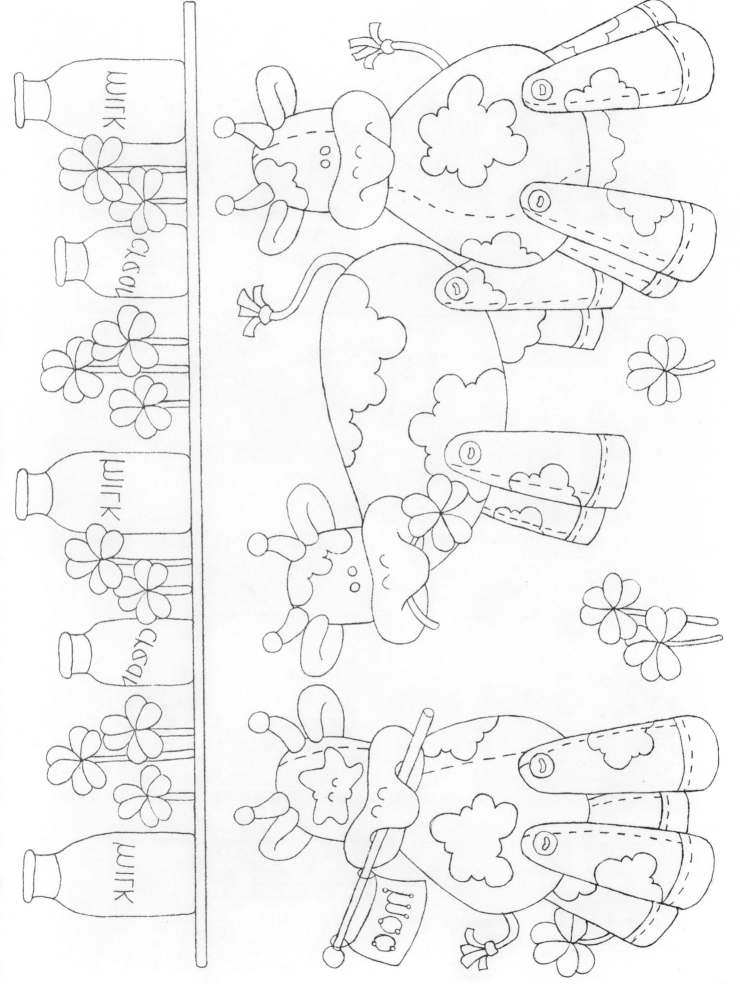

EAT
BEEF

Test
Pattern

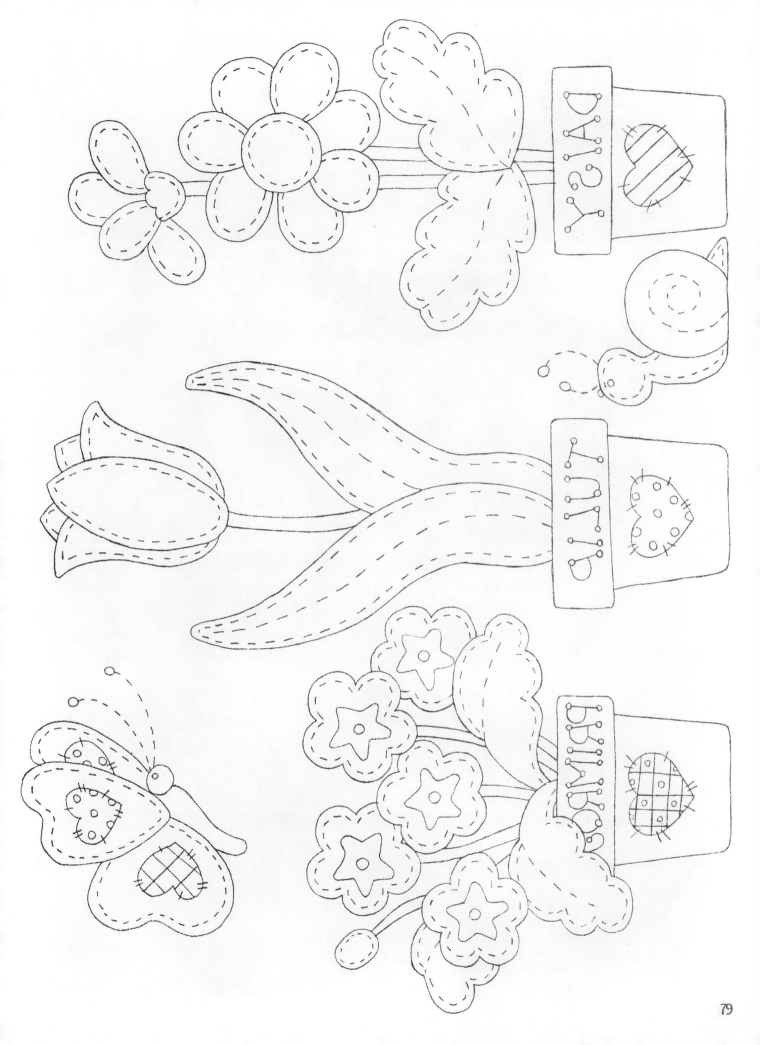

79

WELCOME

Test Pattern

Test
Pattern

85

Test Pattern

89

Test
Pattern

95

BLOOM WHERE YOU'RE
PLANTED

Test Pattern

I ♥ TO GARDEN

CARROTS

WELCOME TO MY PATCH

VIOLET SEEDS

Test
Pattern

GARDENING ANGEL

101

WATERMELON FAIRY

Test Pattern

Test
Pattern

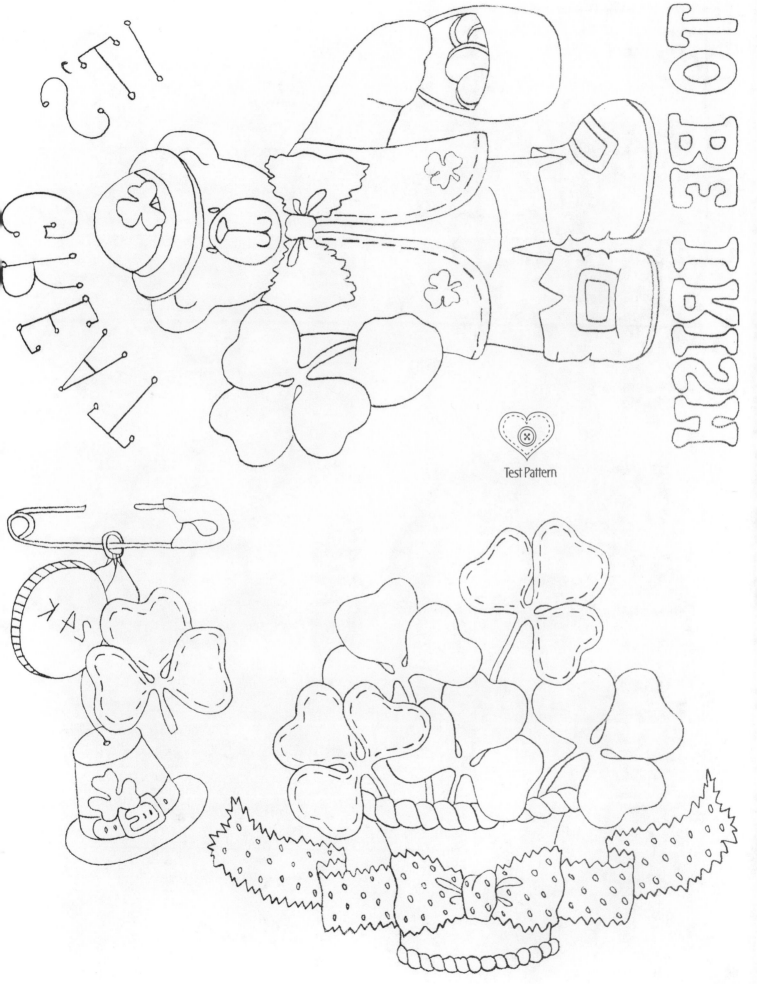

TO BE IRISH

IT'S GREAT

Test Pattern

Test
Pattern

BLESS THE USA

119

GIVE THANKS

Test Pattern

121

Test
Pattern

Test Pattern

131

Test Pattern

Test Pattern

Test
Pattern

151

Test Pattern

155

Test
Pattern

157